The Rosary
A Children's Guide to the Rosary

The Life Story of Jesus Through Mary's Eyes

*Bible quotes from
Douay-Rheims
1899 American Edition*

*Written and Illustrated by
Kelly Lorenzen*

Copyright © 2014 by Kelly Lorenzen
All rights reserved.
ISBN: 0692028188
ISBN-13: 978-0692028186

The First Joyful Mystery
The Annunciation

The angel said to Mary, "Peace be with you. God has chosen you to be the mother of his only son." Mary was scared at first but she put her faith and trust in God and through the Holy Spirit she became pregnant.

Luke 1:26-27 *And in the sixth month, the angel Gabriel was sent from God into a city of Galilee, called Nazareth, to a virgin espoused to a man whose name was Joseph, of the house of David; and the virgin's name was Mary.*

The Second Joyful Mystery
The Visitation

Mary visits her cousin Elizabeth who is also pregnant. Elizabeth is very old and everyone is happy she is pregnant. When Elizabeth hears her voice, St. John moves inside her body and Elizabeth knows Mary is pregnant with someone very special.

Luke 1:41-42   And it came to pass, that when Elizabeth heard the salutation of Mary, the infant leaped in her womb. And Elizabeth was filled with the Holy Ghost: And she cried out with a loud voice, and said: Blessed art thou among women, and blessed is the fruit of thy womb.

The Third Joyful Mystery
The Nativity

Mary and Joseph travel to Bethlehem to be counted with the rest of his family. When they arrive there is no room anywhere for them to stay. Joseph and Mary started to worry because they needed a place for Mary and the baby. Finally, Joseph found a stable and there Mary gave birth to Jesus.

Luke 2:7 *And she brought forth her firstborn son, and wrapped him up in swaddling clothes, and laid him in a manger; because there was no room for them in the inn.*

The Fourth Joyful Mystery
The Presentation of the Child Jesus at the Temple

Joseph and Mary take Jesus to the temple as any good Jewish parents do. While they are there, Simeon realizes he is looking at his savior. He is very happy and thanks God for letting him see his savior.

Luke 2:25-26 And behold there was a man in Jerusalem named Simeon, and this man was just and devout, waiting for the consolation of Israel; and the Holy Ghost was in him. And he had received an answer from the Holy Ghost, that he should not see death, before he had seen the Christ of the Lord.

The Fifth Joyful Mystery
The Finding of the Child Jesus in the Temple

Joseph, Mary and Jesus go on a trip to Jerusalem for a Passover Festival with their friends and family. On the way home they realize Jesus isn't with them anymore. Mary was scared that something had happened to him. They went back to Jerusalem and after three days they found him teaching in the temple. Jesus told them they should have known he would be at his father's house.

Luke 2:46-47 *And it came to pass, that, after three days, they found him in the temple, sitting in the midst of the doctors, hearing them, and asking them questions. And all that heard him were astonished at his wisdom and his answers.*

The First Luminous Mystery
The Baptism of Jesus in the River Jordan

John the Baptist is baptizing people in the River Jordan. Jesus comes to him and asks him to baptize him. John says he's not good enough to baptize Jesus but he listens to Jesus and baptizes him. As Jesus comes out of the water a voice from heaven says, "This is my son."

Matthew 3:16-17 And Jesus being baptized, forthwith came out of the water: and lo, the heavens were opened to him: and he saw the Spirit of God descending as a dove, and coming upon him. And behold a voice from heaven, saying: This is my beloved Son, in whom I am well pleased.

The Second Luminous Mystery
The Wedding at Cana

Jesus and Mary were at a wedding. The wedding party ran out of wine for the guests to drink. Mary came to Jesus and asked him to help. He said, "My time has not yet come." Mary told the servants to do what he asked. They filled the jugs with water and Jesus turned the water into wine. It was a very good wine and everyone was very happy. This was Jesus' first miracle.

John 2:7-10 Jesus saith to them: Fill the waterpots with water. And they filled them up to the brim. And Jesus saith to them: Draw out now, and carry to the chief steward of the feast. And they carried it. And when the chief steward had tasted the water made wine, and knew not whence it was, but the waiters knew who had drawn the water; the chief steward calleth the bridegroom, and saith to him: Every man at first setteth forth good wine, and when men have well drunk, then that which is worse. But thou hast kept the good wine until now.

The Third Luminous Mystery
Jesus preaches the Word of God

Jesus went with his disciples from town to town teaching the people about God. He talked to them about how God wanted them to behave. He also made the sick and the injured better and performed many miracles.

Matthew 4:23 And Jesus went about all Galilee, teaching in their synagogues, and preaching the gospel of the kingdom: and healing all manner of sickness and every infirmity, among the people.

The Fourth Luminous Mystery
The Transfiguration

While he was up on a mountain with some of his disciples Jesus' clothes were turned dazzling white and two glorious men, Moses and Elijah, appeared. The disciples were confused but then Moses and Elijah disappeared and a voice came from the cloud and told them, "This is my son."

Matthew 17:5 And as he was yet speaking, behold a bright cloud overshadowed them. And lo, a voice out of the cloud, saying: This is my beloved Son, in whom I am well pleased: hear ye him.

The Fifth Luminous Mystery
The Institution of the Eucharist

Jesus was celebrating Passover with his apostles and, while they were eating, he turned the bread and wine into his body and blood.

Matthew 26:26-28 And whilst they were at supper, Jesus took bread, and blessed, and broke: and gave to his disciples, and said: Take ye, and eat. This is my body. And taking the chalice, he gave thanks, and gave to them, saying: Drink ye all of this. For this is my blood of the new testament, which shall be shed for many unto remission of sins.

The First Sorrowful Mystery
The Agony in the Garden

Jesus went to pray in the garden of Gethsemane. He knew what was going to happen to him and asked God that he be spared but then he said, "Let your will be done." Judas then betrayed him and gave him up to the chief priests and the elders.

Matthew 26:47-48 As he yet spoke, behold Judas, one of the twelve, came, and with him a great multitude with swords and clubs, sent from the chief priests and the ancients of the people. And he that betrayed him, gave them a sign, saying: Whomsoever I shall kiss, that is he, hold him fast.

The Second Sorrowful Mystery
The Scourging at the Pillar

The chief priests and elders handed Jesus over to the governor, Pontius Pilate. Pontius Pilate did not want to crucify Jesus but he did what the people insisted. Jesus was taken prisoner and tied to a pillar where the guards beat and spit on him.

Mark 14:65 And some began to spit on him, and to cover his face, and to buffet him, and to say unto him: Prophesy: and the servants struck him with the palms of their hands.

The Third Sorrowful Mystery
The Crowning with Thorns

The soldiers made fun of Jesus and dressed him in a purple robe. Then they nailed a crown of thorns upon his head.

John 19:2 And the soldiers platting a crown of thorns, put it upon his head; and they put on him a purple garment.

The Fourth Sorrowful Mystery
The Carrying of the Cross

Jesus is made to carry the cross to the hill of Golgotha to be crucified. He fell three times while carrying the cross and Simon from Cyrene was forced to help him.

John 19:16 17 Then therefore he delivered him to them to be crucified. And they took Jesus, and led him forth. And bearing his own cross, he went forth to that place which is called Calvary, but in Hebrew Golgotha.

The Fifth Sorrowful Mystery
The Crucifixion

After a very painful three hours, Jesus died on the cross with a criminal crucified on each side of him. None of his bones were broken and when a soldier put a lance in his side, blood and water flowed out.

Luke 23:46 And Jesus crying out with a loud voice, said: Father, into thy hands I commend my spirit. And saying this, he gave up the ghost.

The First Glorious Mystery
The Resurrection

When Mary came to the tomb where Jesus was buried she found the tomb empty and the stone rolled back. After three days, Jesus had risen from the dead.

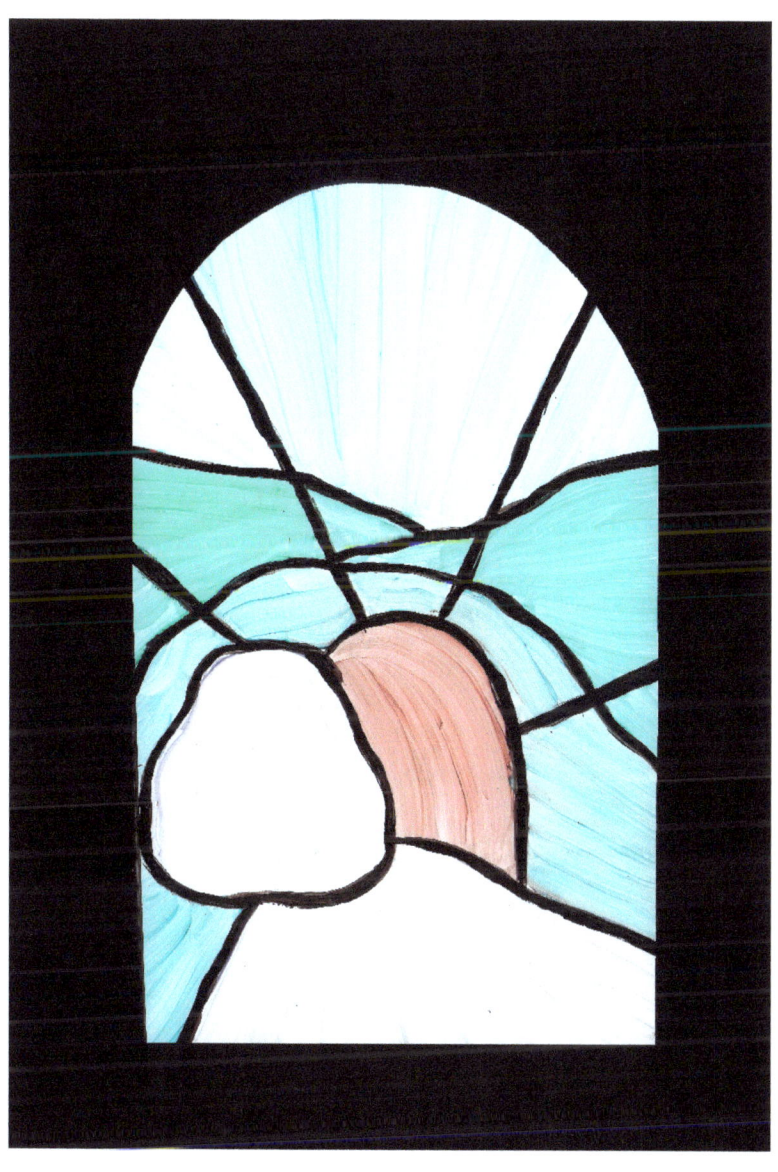

Matthew 28:5-6 And the angel answering, said to the women: Fear not you; for I know that you seek Jesus who was crucified. He is not here, for he is risen, as he said. Come, and see the place where the Lord was laid.

The Second Glorious Mystery
The Ascension

After 40 days, Jesus went into heaven; ready to come again, sometime in the future.

Luke 24:51 *And it came to pass, whilst he blessed them, he departed from them, and was carried up to heaven.*

The Third Glorious Mystery
The Descent of the Holy Spirit Upon the Apostles

The apostles were scared and hiding after Jesus went up into heaven but then Jesus sent the Holy Spirit to them. The Holy Spirit gave them the strength, power and courage they needed to go out and preach the word of the Lord.

Acts 2:4 And they were all filled with the Holy Ghost, and they began to speak with divers tongues, according as the Holy Ghost gave them to speak.

The Fourth Glorious Mystery
The Assumption of the Virgin Mary

Mary left the earth to go to heaven to be with Jesus. She prays for us while she is there.

John 14:3 *And if I shall go, and prepare a place for you, I will come again, and will take you to myself; that where I am, you also may be.*

The fifth Glorious Mystery
The Coronation

Mary is crowned Queen of Heaven. She is seated in Heaven next to her son, Jesus.

Revelation 12:1 And a great sign appeared in heaven: A woman clothed with the sun, and the moon under her feet, and on her head a crown of twelve stars

Prayers of the Rosary

Our Father
Our father who art in heaven hallowed be thy name, thy kingdom come, thy will be done on Earth as it is in Heave, give us this day our daily bread and forgive us our trespasses as we forgive those who trespass against us and lead us not into temptation but deliver us from evil. Amen

Hail Mary
Hail Mary Full of Grace the Lord is with thee, blessed art thou among women and blessed is the fruit of thy womb, Jesus, Holy Mary Mother of God pray for us sinners now and at the hour of our death. Amen.

Glory Be
Glory be to the Father and to the son ,and to the Holy Spirit, as it was in the beginning is now and ever shall be Amen.

Fatima Prayer
O, My Jesus, forgive us our sins, save us from the fires of hell and lead all souls to heaven especially those most in need of thy mercy

Hail Holy Queen

Hail, holy Queen, Mother of Mercy! Our life, our sweetness, and our hope! To thee do we cry, poor banished children of Eve, to thee do we send up our sighs, mourning and weeping in this valley, of tears. Turn, then, most gracious advocate, thine eyes of mercy toward us; and after this our exile show unto us the blessed fruit of thy womb Jesus; O clement, O loving, O sweet virgin Mary, Pray for us, O holy Mother of God That we may be made worthy of the promises of Christ.

The Apostles' Creed

I believe in God the Father Almighty, Creator of heaven and earth; and in Jesus Christ, His only Son, our Lord; Who was conceived by the Holy Spirit, born of the Virgin Mary, suffered under Pontius Pilate, was crucified, died and was buried. He descended into hell. On the third day He arose again; He ascended into heaven and sits at the right hand of God, the Father Almighty; from thence He shall come to judge the living and the dead. I believe in the Holy Spirit, the Holy Catholic Church, the communion of saints, the forgiveness of sins, the resurrection of the body, and life everlasting. Amen

How to Pray the Rosary

Make the Sign of the Cross -Say the Apostles' Creed -Say the Our Father -Say three Hail Marys -Say the Glory be to the Father -Announce the First Mystery -Say the Our Father -Say ten Hail Marys, while meditating on the Mystery -Say the Glory be to the Father and Fatima Prayer -Repeat for the remaining four Mysteries -Close the Rosary with the Hail Holy Queen

www.ingramcontent.com/pod-product-compliance
Lightning Source LLC
Chambersburg PA
CBHW041755040426
42446CB00001B/43